G000277328

G. PIVARD
D. LEMARESQUIER

THE BAYEUX TAPESTRY
narrated to children

OREP
EDITIONS

SUMMARY

Preface 3

Three Kings of England in the year 1066 4

The Story of a Conquest 5

Epilogue 38

Educational booklet 39

    The map 40

    The Bayeux Tapestry 41

    The bestiary 42

    The fables 43

    It's your turn to play... 44

    Games 46

    Glossary of words 47

The pages are colour coded:

 scenes from **Normandy**,

 scenes from **Ponthieu**,

 scenes from **England**,

 war scenes,

 maritime scenes.

This book is designed for children from age 5 upwards.
The story is freely inspired by the Bayeux Tapestry and the historical events are true.

Certain words, followed by an asterisk, are explained on page 47.

Since its revelation by the learned at the dawn of the 18th Century, the Bayeux Tapestry has been the source of several hundred publications by established or amateur historians. Every stitch of it has been scrutinised, but almost always by an adult public. However, for the first time, a book totally devoted to children now explains the story of the Bayeux Tapestry in an educational but also a playful manner. Gilles Pivard, a primary school teacher, and David Lemaresquier, a secondary school art teacher, both have extensive knowledge of this masterpiece. Over several years, they have put their teaching skills into practice within the Bayeux Tapestry Museum's educational department and offer advice to their colleagues wishing to study the tapestry with their pupils. Their complementary contributions, via quality texts and illustrations, offer a very pleasant book for children and adolescents to explore.

Sylvette LEMAGNEN
Bayeux Tapestry Honorary Curator

Three Kings of England in the year 1066

My name is **Edward** the Confessor, because I am a strong Christian believer. I have a magnificent white beard and I'm 60 years old, which is already a great age for the eleventh century. I have been King of England for the last 22 years.

I have just had Westminster Abbey rebuilt and I hope to be buried there.

No children have been born from my marriage with Harold's sister, Edith. There are therefore no heirs to my throne and I am sure that my life is nearing its end.

In 1064, I sent Harold of Wessex, one of my kingdom's most powerful Earls, to tell the Duke of Normandy, William the Bastard, that I wanted him to become King after my death. I thought of him since I spent my childhood in exile in Normandy before becoming king. I am sure that the Duke of Normandy has all the qualities of a good king.

My name is **Harold** of Wessex. I'm 42 years old and I am the son of Godwine, a powerful English Earl. I have long hair and a drooping moustache. I am Earl of Wessex, a rich region in the South of England. I am the head of English aristocracy, in other words, of all of the English lords. I am particularly powerful in the South of England and I have great influence on the decisions of the king, who married my sister, Edith. Very often, I oblige him to make my own political choices.

I was born in England and have the support of the population and the English clerics. In 1064, Edward sent me to deliver an important message to William, the Duke of Normandy.

My name is **William**, nicknamed the Bastard because I was born out of wedlock. I am 37 years old. As is the fashion in Normandy, the nape of my neck is shaved.

In 911, the King of France gave the region of Normandy to my Norwegian ancestor, Rollon. Now I am the region's Duke. Normandy is one of France's most important territorial provinces. The King of France is afraid of me. I am married to Matilda, the daughter of the Count of Flanders, a neighbouring land. My duchy is peaceful and prosperous. I govern it severely and I have a mighty army.

Although I am a stranger to the kingdom of England, its king, my cousin Edward, decided in 1051 that I should succeed him to the throne after his death. What's more, in 1064, he sent Harold to confirm this to me.

The story of a conquest

Rouen - 9th September 1087

'Hello, my name is Turold. I am a poet and a musician. I am so sad: my dear William, Duke of Normandy and King of England has just died! Oh, I had so many great times by his side! I'm going to tell you the story of one of our most extraordinary adventures...'

The story began one morning in the year 1064
in one of the castles of Edward the Confessor, King of England.

Whilst seated on his throne, the King sent for his brother-in-law, Harold of Wessex.

'Harold, I am old and tired. I have an important mission* for you.

Go quickly to Normandy and tell my cousin, the Duke William that he will become King of England upon my death.'

'Noble king, I will abide by your wishes,' replied Harold.

A little later, Harold reunited all of his friends.

'To your horses', he cried, 'We must go to Bosham harbour as quickly as possible!'

Harold, with his falcon on his arm, pushed his horse into a gallop. His hunting dogs, their bells ringing, ran in front of him barking. He thought,
'So, Edward wants to designate William as heir to the English throne! But will the English accept this foreigner as their king?'

DVX·ANGLORVM·ETSVI MILITES·EQV TANT·AD BOS

After praying for a safe voyage in the small church of Bosham, Harold and his companions enjoyed a good meal.

'My friends', exclaimed Harold, 'we have been entrusted with a mission*. Tomorrow, we must take to the seas and perhaps face many dangers. Let us drink to the success of this adventure!'

The following morning, the sun was hidden from view by heavy clouds.

The strident* cries of seagulls could be heard as they flew around the boats. The sea was calm. The men were agitated. Bare-footed, they loaded the last of the baggage and carried their dogs on board.

'Weigh the anchor and hoist the sails', ordered Harold.

The Channel crossing went smoothly until suddenly the sky darkened.

The wind was blowing more and more fiercely and huge waves were forming: a storm was brewing! Would the boat, now severely shaken, be strong enough to resist? The boat was pushed eastwards. The men were afraid. They were frantic, when suddenly, the sailor at the top of the mast, cried, 'Land, land!' And Harold wondered, 'On what coast are we preparing to land?'

Harold had barely set foot on the beach when armed men leaped on him to capture him. He tried to resist, but a horseman approached and said to him,

'Stop struggling. I am Guy de Ponthieu, Count* of this region and you are my prisoner.'

Harold, encircled, had no choice but to surrender.

Harold was taken with his companions
to Guy de Ponthieu's castle.

On the way there, Harold wondered,
'How are we going to escape from this misfortune and take King Edward's
message to Duke William?'

AD BELREM: ET IBI EVM: TENVIT:

Harold was received by the count in the great hall. The count, with his sword pointed towards the sky and his finger pointed towards Harold,

dryly said to him,

'Who are you, you who have landed on my territory?'

'I am Harold, brother-in-law and counsellor to King Edward of England. The storm pushed my vessel onto your coast while I was heading for Normandy to see Duke William.'

'You are my prisoner and you will stay here until a ransom* has been paid for your freedom.' A spy, who was hiding behind a pillar heard the whole conversation and said to himself, 'I must inform William; this news will surely be of interest to him!'

In his castle in Rouen, William was informed of the capture of Harold and his men.

I, Turold, was one of those who were sent to fetch Harold, and, from that moment on, was witness* to the events that followed.

He sent armed horsemen to negotiate with Guy de Ponthieu to obtain their freedom. The Count accepted for Normandy was a powerful neighbouring region.

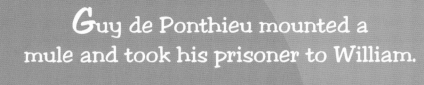

Guy de Ponthieu mounted a mule and took his prisoner to William.

'Look my lord, the Englishman has been treated well.'
'I thank you, Guy, and, in return, please accept my friendship and my protection. As for you, Earl Harold, I wish you welcome to my land, and ask you to accompany us to my great town of Rouen; we will talk there.'

The room's lavish decoration was proof of the Duke's importance and his good taste.

William was peacefully seated in a superb carved chair. An armed guard stood just behind him to protect him. Harold began to tell the story of his voyage but William soon interrupted him and asked,

'Why did my cousin Edward ask you to come to see me?'

'Noble William, my king wishes that, upon his death, you reign over the Kingdom of England.'

William was pleased to learn such news. He exclaimed,

'A powerful land will be born from the allegiance of our territories. As for you, Harold, to seal our friendship, you will go to war with me in Brittany. I must fight Conan, the Count of Rennes.'

A few days later, William's powerful army travelled across Normandy.

As they approached the Mont-Saint-Michel abbey, their horses fell prey to the sinking sand in the bay. Harold, listening only to his courage, leaped onto the sand and managed to save an Englishman and a Norman.

William led his men and attacked Dol Castle.

The battle did not last long.

'Victory, victory!'

cried the Normans when they discovered that Conan had fled with the help of a rope.

William then took control of the town of Rennes before heading for Dinan where his enemy had taken refuge*. The Duke's heavily armed soldiers set fire to the castle.

The besieged* had no choice but to surrender. Conan handed over the town keys, attached to a spearhead, to William.

William was happy, he was victorious.

The Duke then called to Harold on the battlefield and said to him,

'To reward your courage and to prove my friendship to you, I give you my arms. If you remain loyal to me, I will protect you.'

On his return to Normandy, William stopped by to see his half-brother, the bishop* Odo, in Bayeux.

Before returning to England, Harold was to take an oath*
of allegiance to William, over the relics* held in Bayeux Cathedral*.

VBI hAROLD:SACRAMENTVM:FECIT:✓ hIC hAROLD:DVX
VVILLELMO DVCI:-

'I Harold of Wessex, upon the sacred relics of Saint Raven and Saint Rasiphe,
swear loyalty to you and promise to help you to become king upon the death
of Edward. May I be cursed, should I fail to keep this promise!'

Harold returned to England.

During the Channel crossing, he thought
about his trip to Normandy.

'That cunning
Norman tricked me into
taking that oath.'

As soon as he arrived home, King Edward received him in his palace.
'Noble King', said Harold as he bowed before him, 'I took your message
to William.'
'I am relieved', replied Edward, who looked exhausted.

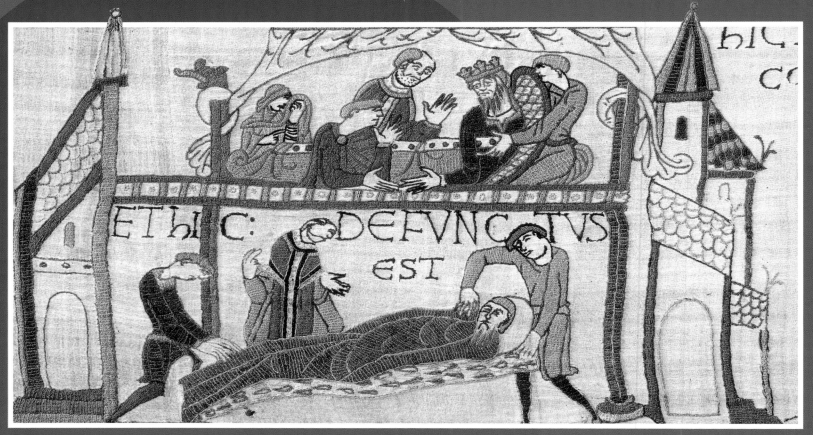

In the silent palace of the King of England, the Queen was heard sobbing while a bishop recited prayers. Edward was dying.

Lying on his deathbed, he whispered to Harold,

'Choose the best route so that England remains united and its people happy.'

Upon these words, the king died while holding out his hand towards Harold.

The powerful English lords met to choose the new king.

They came to see Harold and said to him,

'Take the crown of England. You are the most worthy man to succeed Edward.'

Harold hesitated before such a great honour. To be crowned King of England! His dream!
He replied,
'Yes, I accept to become your king. Thanks be to God, our kingdom will know justice and peace.'

23

In the great hall of the royal palace, Harold was crowned and sat, majestically on his throne.

He was now King of England! He held a sceptre* in his right hand and a globe in his left hand and happily, he listened to the English people shout,

'Long live King Harold, God save England!'

The crowd was full of joy.

Soon afterwards...

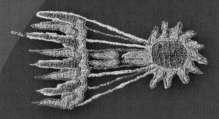

The English noticed a star shooting across the sky at great speed, leaving behind a cloud of fire.

'A comet* is always a sign of misfortune! But what is going to happen to us?' thought the nation anxiously.

King Harold was immediately informed of this strange event.

Spies sent by William were leaving England to tell him of Harold's treachery. As soon as William learned the news, he cried,

'Harold has betrayed his oath; he has taken the crown that should have been mine!'

His brother, Odo, proclaimed,

'He lied before God. He must be punished. William, you must cross the Channel to chase this sinful traitor!'

The Duke of Normandy then reunited his counsellors and ordered,

'My friends, prepare boats and build the greatest fleet that has ever been seen. Build weapons. Gather equipment, horses and foodstuffs. Call up all the men who are ready to fight. Together, we will make Harold pay for his disloyalty.'

26

The agitation spread throughout the entire region of Normandy.

All of the region's lumberjacks and carpenters set to work.
Trees were felled. Planks of wood were prepared to build boats.
The boats were grouped together in the harbour in Dives-sur-Mer.
They then needed to be loaded with horses, weapons and food.
Some men carried the heavy coats of mail and swords, whilst
others pulled carts loaded with spears, helmets and barrels
of wine.

ISTI PORTANT:ARMAS: ADNAVES: ETHIC TRAHVNT:CARRVM CVM VINO:ET ARMIS:

NAVIGIO: MAR E TRAN SIMI

And thanks to favourable winds, thousands of William's warriors reached Saint-Valery in the Somme Bay. A few days later, they finally crossed the Channel in only one night.
Aboard his vessel, the Mora, the Duke wondered,

'What does the future hold? Will we win this battle or will we all die?'

The only reply he heard was the noise of the waves on the hull of his boat.

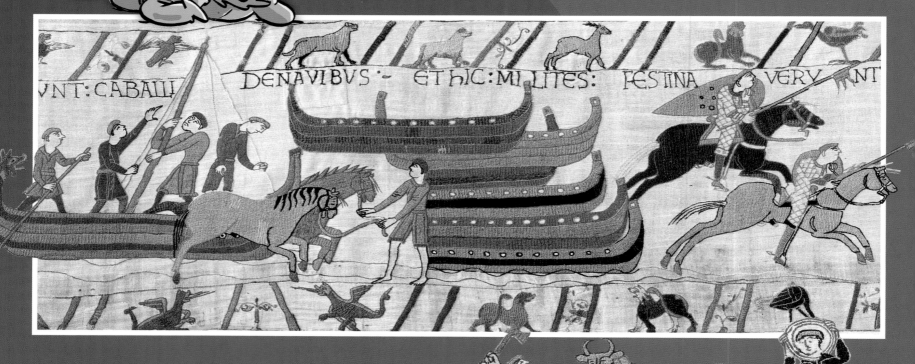

Early in the morning, the Normans landed on English soil. Pathfinders* on horseback explored the surroundings and stole livestock from local farmers to feed the soldiers.

The men were hungry!

The cooks prepared a magnificent banquet. Meat was roasted above large bonfires. The soldiers used their shields as plates. Further away, at the great table where the Duke sat, the barons listened to Bishop Odo as he blessed* the meal. With his hand raised, Robert of Mortain, William's younger brother exclaimed,

'Let us eat quickly and prepare our battle plan!'

The Normans built a huge fortified camp near Hastings. They dug ditches and a feudal motte* was erected. A wooden tower was built on its summit.

Thousands of men were rushing around. Some of them looked after the horses, others trained for combat.

William and his two brothers were preparing their battle plan when, suddenly, a pathfinder emerged, breathless,

'My lords, Harold's army is approaching and will soon be here.'

The Duke of Normandy stood up and made the following declaration,

'I want all of the houses that might hinder us on the battlefield to be burned.'

14th October 1066

At dawn, William gathered together his mighty army. The Duke encouraged his men before the fighting commenced,

'My friends, we can no longer turn back. Let us fight with wrath to destroy the enemy. Let us advance, and may God protect us!'

The English watchmen* who were hiding in the trees could not believe their eyes,

'They are attacking, we must inform the king!' they cried.

The Norman horsemen brandishing their javelins*, launched their attack on the hill where Harold's men were entrenched. The whistling sound of arrows could be heard all around.

The English, who were on foot, resisted and managed to fend off the enemy several times.

They slashed the horses with their large axes. The combat was violent and blood was flowing. Arms and legs were chopped off. Many soldiers were killed. Harold's two brothers were among the dead.

The fighting was so violent that it was impossible to tell friend from foe.

Suddenly, the Norman army was panic-stricken. William had disappeared. Was he dead? Discouraged, the Normans started to retreat. Then a horseman lifted his helmet, it was William! He yelled, 'I am here, and I am alive! Be brave, God will grant us victory! Let us attack without respite and without pity!'
Accordingly, all of the Normans regained confidence and plunged into the enemy with rage.

After several hours of combat...

The English soldiers were exhausted. Showers of arrows were rushing down on them. King Harold, upright next to his red dragon standard, courageously resisted when an arrow struck his eye. He suffered terribly. At that precise instant, four Norman horsemen sprung on him and chopped him into pieces. William was the master of the battlefield where plunderers were already removing coats of mail and weapons from many of the dead.

Without their chief, the English were totally disheartened and fled, pursued by the pitiless Norman soldiers. It was a stampede!

William was the conqueror. He could now become King of England.

'I Turold, will never forget the great ceremony in Westminster Abbey, when on Christmas day 1066, William of Normandy was crowned King of England.
I will always remember that glorious adventure from my childhood: the conquest of the kingdom of England by the Normans, just like the story related on the magnificent Bayeux Tapestry!'

Educational booklet

The map 40

The Bayeux Tapestry 41

The bestiary 42

The fables 43

It's your turn to play... 44

Games 46

Glossary of words 47

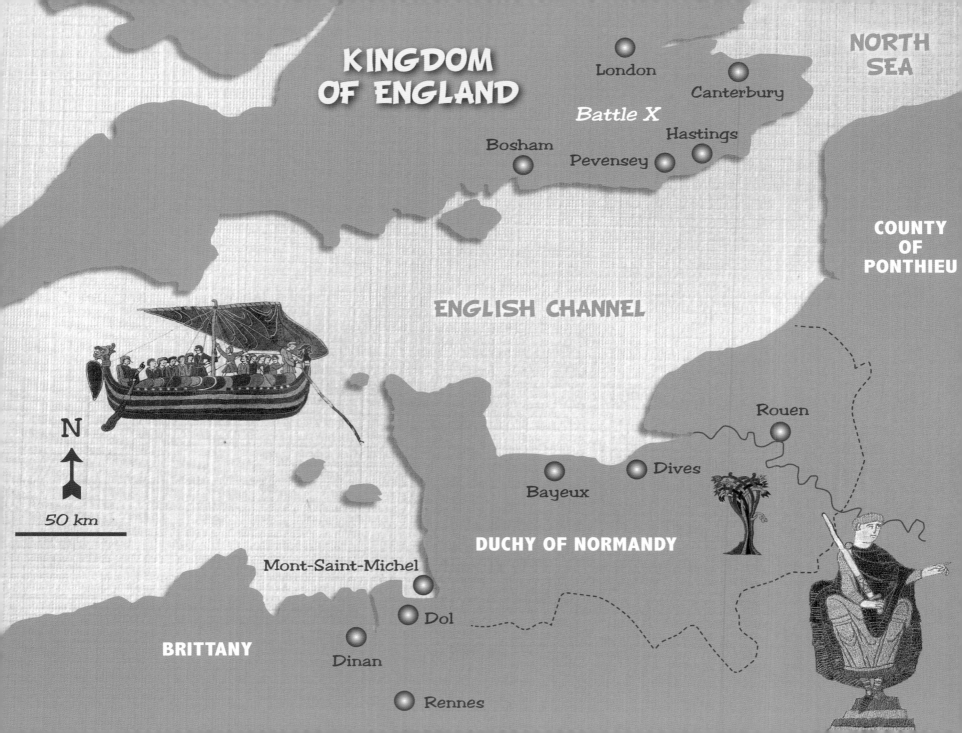

KINGDOM
OF ENGLAND

NORTH
SEA

London

Canterbury

Battle X

Bosham

Hastings

Pevensey

COUNTY
OF
PONTHIEU

ENGLISH CHANNEL

Rouen

N

Dives

Bayeux

50 km

DUCHY OF NORMANDY

Mont-Saint-Michel

Dol

BRITTANY

Dinan

Rennes

The Bayeux Embroidery

The **Bayeux Tapestry** is a unique masterpiece embroidered in the 11th Century. It is nearly a thousand years old! It is an embroidery measuring nearly 70 metres long and 50 centimetres high. It was sewn on a strip of linen fabric using needles and dyed wool. In a series of picture images, it tells the story of the conquest of England by William, Duke of Normandy, in 1066.

Contrary to the name given to the embroidery from the 18th century, when study began on the work, Queen Matilda's Tapestry was not embroidered by William the Conqueror's wife. The Bishop of Bayeux, Odo of Conteville, and also William's half-brother, is said to have ordered the tapestry from an English embroidery workshop in Canterbury.

The tapestry may have been displayed for the first time in the nave of Bayeux Cathedral on the 14th of July 1077.

It was designed to be displayed in order to justify William's expedition across the Channel. The English Earl Harold is said to have breached the oath he took over sacred relics, swearing that, after Edward's death, he would leave the throne of England to William. It is believed that, for this sin, God punished Harold, who was killed during the Battle of Hastings on the 14th of October 1066.

The Bestiary

Each of them approximately 7cm large, the upper and lower borders of the **Bayeux Tapestry** include many genuine animals such as lions, birds and even camels, but also legendary creatures (also known as fantastic, fabulous or mythical beasts) such as griffins, dragons or centaurs.

Separated by single or double oblique strokes, these creatures walk either in the same or in opposite directions. When they walk in opposite directions, they are almost perfectly symmetrical, as if they were looking in a mirror.

Fables

In the Bayeux Tapestry's border, ancient fables are also depicted. A fable is a short tale relating a general reality and often ending in a moral. These fables were written by the fabulist, Phedrus in the 1st century AD. They were revived in the 17th Century by Jean de La Fontaine. It is quite amusing to try to identify fables such as 'The Crow and the Fox' or 'The Wolf and the Lamb'...

Now it's your turn to play
Try to answer the following questions

Question 1

What historical event is related on the Bayeux Tapestry?
   a) Bonaparte's attempted invasion of England in 1804
  b) The allied D-Day landings on the Normandy beaches in 1944
  c) William the Conqueror's conquest of England in 1066

Question 2

Who tells the story in this book?
a) Harold
b) Turold
c) William

Question 3

What was the relationship between King Edward and Harold?
a) They were brothers
b) They were brothers-in-law
c) They were cousins

Question 4

Where did Harold land at the beginning of the story?
a) In Normandy
b) In Brittany
c) In Ponthieu

Question 5

What message did Harold take to William?
a) Edward had declared war against William
b) Edward wished for William to succeed him to the throne
c) Edward had invited William to go to his palace in England

Question 6

What happened in the Mont-Saint-Michel bay?
a) Just in time, Harold saved soldiers from the sinking sand
b) William's army was attacked by Bretons
c) William and Harold ate an omelette

Question 7

What was the Count of Rennes' name?
a) Ronan
b) Arthur
c) Conan

Question 8

In what order did William attack the Breton towns?
a) Dinan, Dol, Rennes
b) Dol, Rennes, Dinan
c) Dol, Dinan, Rennes

Question 9

Who was Odo?
a) The Bishop of Bayeux
b) The Count of Ponthieu
c) The Count of Flanders

Question 10

On his return from Brittany, in which town did Harold take an oath?
a) Hastings
b) Rouen
c) Bayeux

Question 11

When he took his oath, what did he swear on?
a) Relics
b) The Bible
c) His parents' life

Question 12

What is the name of the sea that separates Normandy from England?
a) The Black Sea
b) The Mediterranean
c) The English Channel

Question 13

What appeared in the sky after Harold's coronation?
a) A flying saucer
b) The hand of God
c) A comet

Question 14

What did William do when he learned of Harold's coronation?
a) He prepared a military expedition
b) He sent boats loaded with gifts to congratulate him
c) He decided to abandon his claim to the English throne

Question 15

What was the name of William's boat?
a) The Normandy
b) The Conqueror
c) The Mora

Question 16

What did the Normans do after landing in England?
a) They made a giant sandcastle
b) They prepared a huge banquet
c) They immediately returned home

Question 17

How was Harold wounded on the battlefield?
a) He was struck in the eye by an arrow
b) He was impaled by a javelin
c) He was knocked over by a cannonball

Question 18

On what date was William crowned King of England?
a) At Easter 1067
b) At Christmas 1066
c) On the 14th of July 1077

Question 19

What is the Bayeux Tapestry?
a) A wool embroidery on a linen fabric
b) An oil-painting on a wooden frame
c) Photographs stuck on a piece of parchment

Question 20

Who made the Bayeux Tapestry?
a) An embroidery workshop in Canterbury
b) Queen Matilda, helped by her ladies.
c) Odo, the Bishop of Bayeux

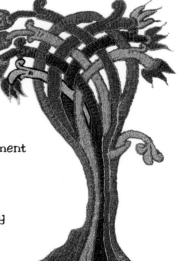

Find the 7 deliberate mistakes

These Englishmen are joyfully celebrating Harold's coronation. But, when they look in the mirror, they discover, in their reflection, 7 mistakes!

a.
a spade

b.
an arrow

c.
a royal globe

d.
a bow

e.
a lumberjack's axe

I've lost something!

These 5 characters from the Bayeux Tapestry have all lost something. Can you find the lost objects…

A labyrinth

This knight would like to return to his castle, but beware of ferocious beasts! He must avoid them!

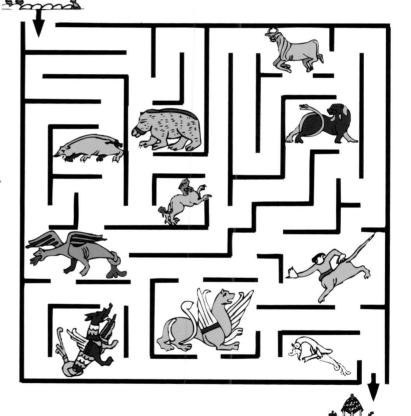

Glossary of words

besieged: soldiers (the besiegers) encircle (besiege) a castle to force its occupants (the *besieged*) to surrender.

a bishop: administers a diocese: he is the head priest. His place of residence is called the bishop's palace.

bless: during a ceremony, the priest/minister *blesses* the faithful: he asks God to protect them, he gives them his benediction.

a cathedral: is a large church headed by a bishop. The bishop's throne, his cathedra, can be found there.

a comet: is a star that crosses the sky leaving behind a trail of light; it is also called a shooting star.

a count: is a lord, a nobleman, who administers a county, a land that has been entrusted to him by a king or a duke.

a feudal motte: the very first wooden fortified castles were built on a large mound of earth, a *motte* that was built and surrounded by trenches called moats.

a javelin: is a sort of spear that can be thrown a great distance.

a mission: this soldier's *mission* is to watch over the enemy: it's the job he's been given.

an oath: is a solemn promise. To take an *oath,* is to swear something. To break an oath is called perjury.

a pathfinder: is a soldier who goes in front of the others to watch the enemy approach. He goes out to investigate and find out what's ahead.

a ransom: is money demanded in return for someone's freedom.

a relic: is part of a saint's body or an object belonging to him/her that is preserved and highly respected. It is a sacred object.

a sceptre: is a sort of stick held by a king and signifying his power.

strident: a *strident* cry is a shrill, piercing cry.

to take refuge: is to take shelter somewhere else.

a watchman: is the man who, from his post on the castle ramparts, watches over the surrounding area.

a witness: is someone who has taken part in an event.

Acknowledgments

David Lemaresquier dedicates this book to Simone Laurence, his grandmother,
and Gilles Pivard to Thomas, his son.
They also thank all those who have contributed to the completion of this book, and in particular:
Sylvette Lemagnen, Honorary curator of the Bayeux media library and of the Bayeux Tapestry
Isabelle Robert, Former Director of the Bayeux Tapestry Museum
Annick Léonard, Former manager of the youth section of the Bayeux media library
and the town of Bayeux...

Answers:

Pages 44 and 45: 1-c; 2-b; 3-b; 4-c; 5-b; 6-a; 7-c; 8-b; 9-a; 10-c; 11-a; 12-c; 13-c;
14-a; 15-c; 16-b; 17-a; 18-b; 19-a; 20-a

Page 46 : Find the 7 deliberate mistakes: an extra leg; an extra hand; an extra head;
one of the characters has a shaved crown; a missing head; a hand is closed.
I lost something! 1-e; 2-c; 3-a; 4-b; 5-d

OREP Éditions, Zone tertiaire de Nonant, 14400 BAYEUX - **Tel.:** 02 31 51 81 31 - **Fax:** 02 31 51 81 32
E-mail: info@orepeditions.com - **Web:** www.orepeditions.com - **Editor:** Grégory Pique - **English Translation:** Heather Inglis
Proofreading: Joëlle Meudic/Heather Inglis - **Graphic design, layout:** Sophie Youf - **Turold illustrations:** Régis Hector
ISBN: 978-2-8151-0503-3 - © OREP Éditions 2023 - All rights reserved - **Legal deposit:** 2006.
In accordance with the French law n° 49-956 dated 16th July 1949 on publications for young readers.
Reproduction of illustrations of the Bayeux Tapestry courtesy of the Bayeux Town Council.